Implementing Personalised Care Planning in Long Term Conditions

A Successful Diabetes Handbook

Rosie Walker
Jill Rodgers

Copyright © 2011 Rosie Walker and Jill Rodgers

This publication is protected under the Copyright, Designs and Patents Act 1988.

All rights reserved including re-sale rights. No part of this publication may be reproduced, stored in a retrieval system or transmitted in any form or by any means, electronic, mechanical, photocopying, recording, scanning, or otherwise, without the prior written permission of the copyright owners. All enquiries regarding reuse of any part of this book should be directed to the publishers, SD Publications.

Published by SD Publications, Successful Diabetes, PO Box 819, Northampton NN4 4AG

ISBN 978-1-4477-9371-7

Contents

	Page number
About us	7
Introduction	9

Section 1: An overview of Personalised Care Planning

Chapter 1: PCP explained — 12

What is PCP?	12
Embracing the philosophy of PCP	15
Challenging traditional health service provision	16
Terminology – planning care or care planning?	17

Chapter 2: The background for PCP — 18

PCP and UK health policy	18
Evidence supporting PCP	21
Helping people help themselves	23

Chapter 3: Embedding PCP in health professional practice — 25

PCP and health professional practice	25
Questions for reflection	28

Section 2: Practical Personalised Care Planning

Chapter 4: Preparation for introducing PCP — 32

PCP implementation strategy options	32
Raising awareness	32

Contents (continued)

	Page Number
Chapter 5: PCP interventions	**35**
Tests and investigations prior to the PCP consultation	35
Preparing for the PCP consultation	37
The PCP consultation	39
A five step person centred model of consulting	40
Skills for person centred consulting	45
Additional tips for successful PCP consultations	49

Section 3: Infrastructure for Personalised Care Planning

Chapter 6: Documentation	**52**
An overview of PCP documentation	52
Wording for appointment invitations	54
Wording for results letters	55
Documenting the care plan	57

Chapter 7: Quality assurance	**59**
The main principles of quality assurance (QA)	59
Identifying QA standards and measures	60
The QA process	61

Contents (continued)

Page number

Section 4: Making a Success of Personalised Care Planning

Chapter 8: PCP concerns and questions — **64**
PCP concerns — 64
Frequently asked questions — 66

Chapter 9: Additional resources — **69**
Long term conditions support and campaigning organisations — 69
PCP and diabetes — 69
PCP and long term conditions — 70
Person centred models and consultation skills — 71
Successful Diabetes resources — 72
UK health policy and PCP — 72

References — **73**

About Us

Successful Diabetes is an independent company run by health professionals who are education specialists. We provide products and services to benefit those working or living with diabetes and other long term conditions.

We offer a range of products including books, ebooks and website resources such as recipes and practical tips along with news and comment on key issues as they arise. We also provide learner-centred and skills-based training, including a range of workshops for services wishing to implement the personalised care planning approach.

The authors of this book are Rosie Walker and Jill Rodgers, the Directors of Successful Diabetes.

Introduction

Welcome. This book is for you if you are interested in finding out more or want to become involved in implementing a Personalised Care Planning approach for people with long term conditions. Personalised Care Planning (PCP) is the term used by the UK Department of Health for a holistic process which supports an individual to make choices and achieve their personal goals for their health and well being. This book will provide you with information, guidance, ideas and tips all gained from real life experiences, to help you understand PCP and be able to develop services designed to achieve it.

A good friend of ours who has lived with Type 1 diabetes for several decades once commented "diabetes is a marathon, not a sprint: I need help to stay in the race". These words have shaped our perception of the long journey people travel when they have diabetes or any other long term condition. They have also reminded us that the role of the healthcare professional in long term condition services is much more that of a helper, supporter and facilitator – keeping people in the race – than it is an advisor, care giver or expert consultant. Just as a sprint is very different from a marathon, so the skills needed to complete each are different. Applying this analogy to healthcare, the skills and processes needed to deal with long term conditions are very different from those needed for acute illnesses.

PCP, and all it involves, acknowledges and addresses the different approach needed in long term conditions, which account for the majority of care needs and currently use 70% of healthcare resources in the UK (de Silva, 2011). The idea of care planning and the use of care plans have been around for many years in the NHS, but the newer version of PCP is based on the reality that people with long term conditions make all the decisions about their day to day care and therefore need to experience services which acknowledge, value, support and respect their decision making. We have been delighted that this approach, which we have advocated for many years, is now enshrined in UK health policy and being adopted widely.

This book does not present the argument for the PCP approach: the case for PCP has already been made, and we have included chapters on the background and evidence for PCP, along with a comprehensive reference and further reading section. It has been amply demonstrated that it is an appropriate model to use for the vast majority of routine consultations and annual reviews for people with long term conditions. This book is primarily about implementation, for those beginning to deliver the PCP approach, whether within your own practice, a specialist service or across a health organisation.

We have had the privilege of being involved in helping health organisations with their training and preparations for implementing the PCP approach, both in adopting a district-wide approach and in more cautiously experimenting in individual clinics or surgeries. We pay tribute to these services and we're pleased to share in these pages some of the additional insights this work has given us about the nature of person centred practice.

Implementing PCP will help you to enhance the experience of people living with long term conditions and truly help them to 'stay in the race'. This book will provide you with practical support and help, and we wish you well in your journey.

Section one

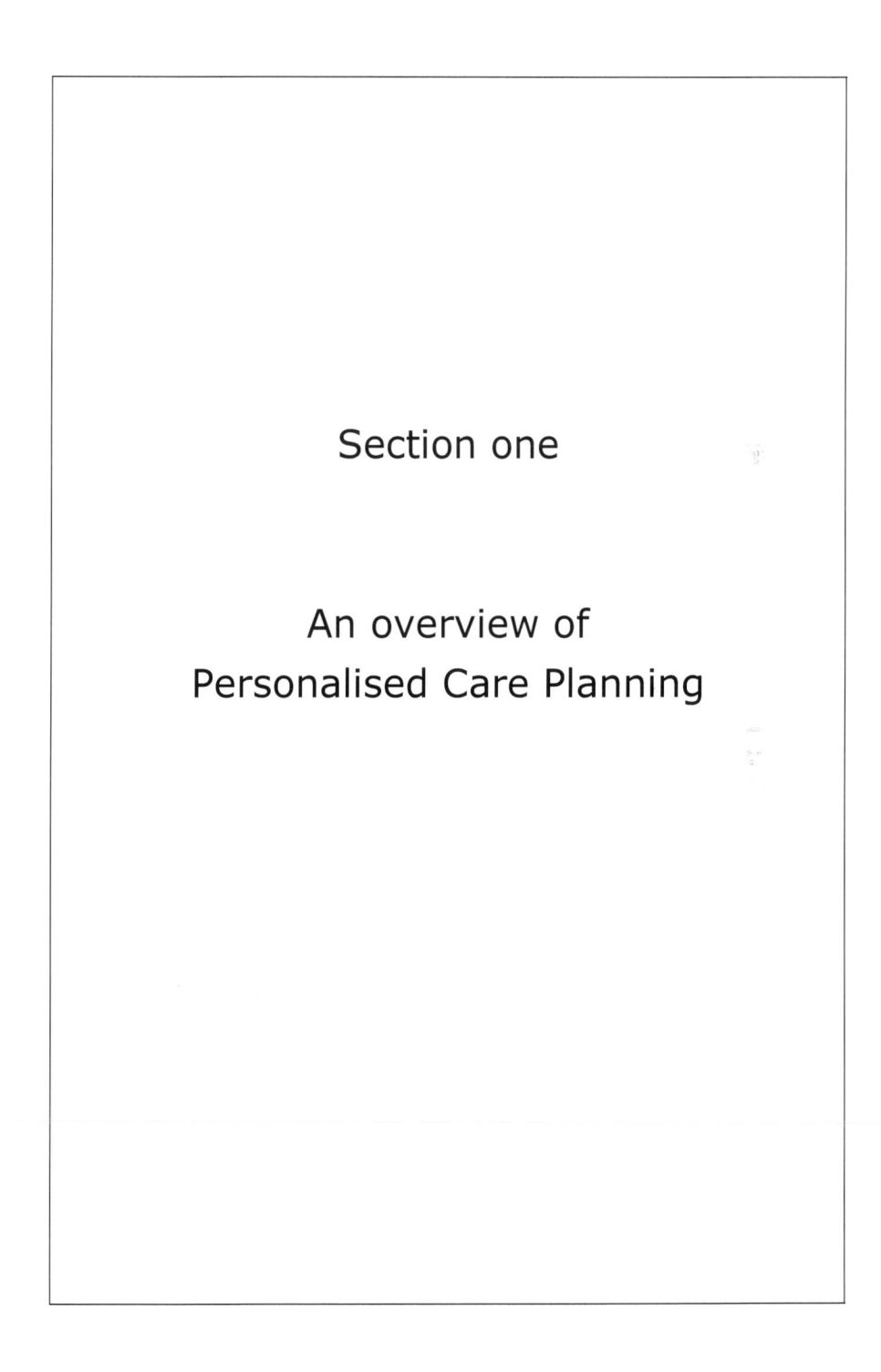

An overview of Personalised Care Planning

Chapter 1: PCP explained

This chapter provides you with an explanation of what PCP is and shows you how the process works in practice. It also identifies some of the fundamental principles embedded in this approach, and how you can meet the challenge of implementing it in the face of traditional service provision.

What is PCP?

'Talk with me, not at me' was the reply from a person with Type 2 diabetes who was asked what would improve his consultations with the health professionals he sees. These words capture exactly what PCP is all about, that is, using a person's experiences of their lives, plus their understanding, thoughts, feelings and wishes about their condition and its care, and keeping all of those aspects at the centre of the service provided for that person.

PCP is a way of recognising that people with long term conditions are responsible for the day to day decisions that affect their condition and that the time they spend with health professionals is very short. This means that their consultations need to be focused on supporting and building up their knowledge and confidence to make everyday decisions, rather than simply being a time when the health professional gives advice or instructions. PCP also includes recognising that providing people with information about their condition, and expecting them to absorb this information and make decisions about their care at the same time, is highly unlikely to be successful.

The way that PCP recognises the reality described above is through a new clinical process, which includes changing the system in which care is provided. The process starts with raising awareness among people with long term conditions about the new system. Following this, the collection of medical information such as blood tests, examinations and investigations happens at an earlier time than the consultation where the results and their implications are discussed. In between these two occasions, the test, examination and investigation results are all provided to the person with the long term condition, together with an objective explanation of what they mean, so that they have time to consider them in advance of their consultation. The person also receives an invitation to reflect on their own priorities, wishes and needs in relation to their condition, including what questions they may have, in preparation for their consultation. If there are no results to share for a particular condition, the person would still receive the invitation to reflect as this is a key part of preparation for participation in PCP.

As a result of the above process, the PCP consultation becomes a collaborative conversation dedicated to discussing the long term condition from the perspective of the person living with it, and their carers where relevant. Their reflections and concerns are the starting point to identifying the person's goal or goals and agreeing an action plan, or personalised care plan, to achieve these.

So it is the process which defines PCP, including the major involvement of the person with the condition, rather than the focus simply being on the generation of a care plan.

> **Successful Diabetes Tip**
>
> Always keep in mind that personalised care planning is a process, quite different from the traditional approach of issuing a care plan

Table 1 overleaf shows the PCP process in full, including the timescales needed to make it work most effectively.

Table 1: A flow diagram showing the key elements of PCP

Before the system is put into place	Raise awareness among people with long term conditions about the change in the system of care.

⬇

About 6-8 weeks prior to the consultation:	Appointment letters sent to individuals, to include the way their appointments will work.

⬇

About 4 weeks prior to the consultation:	Person attends for relevant tests and investigations to be performed or recent results collected.

⬇

About 2 weeks prior to the consultation:	Test results and explanations are shared with person (by letter, email, telephone or collected in person), including prompts and questions for the person to reflect on their results.
	Also included is an invitation to reflect on their own priorities and questions in relation to their life with their long term condition, to discuss in the forthcoming PCP consultation.

⬇

The Personalised Care Planning Consultation:	Sharing of priorities, concerns and thoughts, resulting in an agreed and shared personalised care plan. This includes a plan for follow-up.

⬇

Post consultation:	Activation of the personalised care plan actions, and review as agreed.

Embracing the philosophy of PCP

The most important aspect of PCP is the underlying philosophy that people with long term conditions, not health professionals, are in charge of the day to day decisions about their health. If this philosophy is not followed, it is impossible to implement PCP successfully.

This philosophy can cause some discomfort, such as a perception that people may not appear to participate fully in the PCP, which is often cited as a reason why it should not be fully implemented. But it is important to recognise that any reorganisation to an established system, particularly one which brings such dramatic role changes and expectations, will take time to become established, and there may be caution and concerns expressed by all involved (see concerns and questions, chapter eight).

From a health professional or commissioning perspective, the key to success is putting aside any preconceptions of how someone with a long term condition will respond to the PCP process, for example whether or not they will wish to consider their results and priorities in advance of the PCP consultation, or if they will choose to participate in the PCP consultation or not. The commitment to the philosophy of PCP and the way in which it is implemented will make all the difference to how it is accepted by all parties.

> **Successful Diabetes Tip**
>
> Experimenting with PCP on a small scale will give you some practical experience to reflect on your beliefs and attitudes about it

Challenging traditional health service provision

Whilst the philosophy of PCP is clear, creating expectations of being more involved among people with long term conditions is a major challenge. Health services in the UK traditionally tend to be paternalistic and disempowering. This includes health professionals being seen as the main decision makers in all aspects of health, and the recipients of their services, people who are perfectly capable of being involved, are often made passive. This model of care reflects the historical role of healthcare as providing acute and emergency care.

As healthcare takes account of the increasing prevalence of long term conditions which are largely self managed, so a mismatch has arisen, where the model of care provision is no longer suited to people's needs. The system needs to change to help people be more active in their own care, which is a very important part of implementing PCP and can be done in very practical ways. Examples include inviting people to choose their appointment date and time, taking their own height, weight and blood pressure measurements, or designing their own action plan recording system. In a consultation, change can be effected by prioritising the questions of people with long term conditions, ensuring they have a chance to express their views and wishes and clarifying what they understand by their treatment. All of these will contribute to creating an environment which supports PCP.

> **Successful Diabetes Tip**
> Identify what you are currently doing for people that they could do for themselves, in order to increase their involvement and control in relation to their condition

Terminology – planning care or care planning?

Even though they sound similar and familiar, the term PCP should not be confused with the term 'care plan'. The latter is a term well known to most health professionals who trained in a hospital environment or who provide acute care in the community to those with complex needs or mental health conditions. This type of care plan is traditionally developed by healthcare staff to ensure continuity of care for people who have been admitted to hospital or who need nursing or medical care at home. A care plan produced in this way and for this purpose will be the result of a health or social care professional 'planning care', and as suggested by the term, the onus is on the health professional's responsibilities and decision making.

By contrast, 'care planning' is a much more collaborative approach and it is the process of care planning which holds as much importance as the resulting care plan. Reminding yourself to use this simple change in the order of words will make a difference to how you think about and implement PCP.

The same approach can be applied to two other key concepts in PCP – goal setting and action planning. These mean very different things to 'setting goals' and 'planning action' and thinking about them differently, as above, can also be an effective step on the road to implementation.

> **Successful Diabetes Tip**
>
> Make a conscious effort to notice your terminology in relation to 'care planning', 'goal setting' and 'action planning' and change it if necessary – it will soon become more familiar

Chapter 2: The background for PCP

This chapter shows how PCP fits with health policy within the UK, and also gives an overview of the evidence base for PCP.

PCP and UK Health Policy

Health care in the UK, as in other parts of the world, has changed radically in terms of the challenges it now needs to meet. Providing healthcare to a population which is living longer, where the 30% of people living with long term conditions take up 70% of total NHS resources (de Silva, 2011), is a challenge. This provides a political and financial impetus for people to be more involved in their healthcare, to reduce the burden on the NHS.

It is also important to recognise that in terms of healthcare, a paternalistic approach to health is not fit for purpose in today's world, where web-based information is widely accessed and where choice and individuality are important aspects of everyday life. Both of these dimensions mean that maintaining and promoting personal responsibility is a fitting way forward.

Over the last ten or more years, a succession of health policy has prioritised a personalised approach, which promotes healthier choices, self management of long term conditions and greater involvement and control over decision making by individuals in healthcare settings. Examples include the NHS Plan in 2000, (Department of Health, 2000), which advocated offering 'a personalised service...by 2010 it will be commonplace' (p.17). From this came easier access to health services through conveniently located walk-in centres, a series of national service frameworks addressing the needs of people living with specific long term conditions, and recommendations that people should receive copies of letters about their care and more information about how to choose a GP.

A later publication, 'Our Health, Our Care, Our Say' (DH, 2006a), emphasised that individual's choices about what services they wished for should be prioritised, including, in some cases, the choice about how to spend their personal healthcare budget.

User Involvement has also been strongly championed over the years, with statutory provision made for health organisations to consult and refer to service users about service provision. Supporting literature, websites and information and courses for people who wished to take more control over their health and wellbeing have also expanded, including the NHS website being rebranded 'NHS Choices' (NHS, 2011).

Diabetes was seen as an example of how greater involvement of people in their care could be achieved. The National Service Framework (NSF) for diabetes delivery strategy was published in 2002 (Department of Health, 2002). It put forward a model of 'supported self management' and one of its standards was that every person with diabetes would be much more involved in the decisions made about their care and would be offered a personalised care plan. The report 'Care Planning in Diabetes' followed (Department of Health, 2006b). This described in more detail what a personalised care plan would involve, including the idea of sharing results and inviting people to reflect prior to their annual review or PCP consultation.

The NSF for diabetes set the scene for diabetes to be selected in 2008 as the example long term condition for a 3 year pilot project known as 'Year of Care' to test out the idea of personalised care planning (Health Foundation, 2011). Year of Care includes the care planning approach, plus a linked approach to commissioning a 'menu' of services which is contributed to by people with diabetes. The Year of Care project aimed to show the costs and benefits of a complete year of care for an individual and the value of a transformed clinical method for annual reviews, namely PCP.

The Year of Care report, published in the same month as this book, identifies that the process of PCP is either cost-neutral or can generate cost savings for health services. It also shows that people with diabetes have a better experience of care and make real changes in self-care behaviour. Importantly, a PCP approach has also been well received by health professionals and improved their motivation and understanding of the intricacies of living with a long term condition as well as reducing demand on NHS services (Diabetes UK et al, 2011).

Diabetes was used as the example long term condition for the Year of Care project, but PCP is recommended for use with all long term conditions. 'High Quality Care for All' (Department of Health, 2008), explicitly stated that all people with a long term condition should receive a personalised care plan. Many policy and advisory documents relating to implementing this have subsequently been published for both practitioners and commissioners, including:

* A service specification for personalised care planning (NHS Primary Care Commissioning, 2009)
* Guidance on supporting self management of people with diabetes (Diabetes UK, 2009)
* Information on commissioning personalised care planning (Department of Health, 2009)
* Information for health professionals (NHS Diabetes, 2008)

The personalised approach in general, and PCP in particular, are likely to continue to be recommended, with the most recent health policy White Paper 'Equity and Excellence: liberating the NHS' (Department of Health, 2010) using the term 'no decision about me, without me' to express the importance the current Government attaches to this aspect of healthcare.

The National Institute for Health and Clinical Excellence (NICE) has for some time carried a standard message in every publication about the importance of people's individual needs and preferences being considered and of the person making informed choices, for example in the guidance on adherence to medications (NICE, 2009). The Government has also invested in NICE the responsibility of publishing quality standards for key healthcare issues, including for adults with diabetes. These were published in early 2011 (NICE, 2011). Quality statement 3 reads 'people with diabetes participate in care planning which leads to documented agreed goals and an action plan' (p.4).

Elsewhere in the UK, the devolved Governments of Scotland, Northern Ireland and Wales have also stated their commitment to a person centred philosophy and the need for personalised care plans in supporting people living with long term conditions. They all also recognise that a new approach is needed to address the needs of people with long term conditions, which now form the majority of health care needs (Northern Ireland Department of Health, Social Services and Public Safety, 2011; Scottish Government, 2010; Welsh Assembly Government, 2002).

Evidence supporting PCP

As already highlighted, the Year of Care project (NHS Diabetes, 2011) has tested the PCP pathway, including commissioning, with positive outcomes in terms of systems, processes, acceptability and experience of health services. Other research into the project, including the medical, psychological and sociological perspectives, is ongoing. However, there is already a great deal of useful evidence for a more person centred approach in general, and for the individual components of PCP such as advance preparation for the consultation and the use of goal setting and action planning.

The benefits of people's greater participation in decision making on health outcomes have been shown for many years, particularly in long term conditions. Greater control of a consultation by the person, in terms of asking questions and gaining information for example, showed improvements in blood pressure and blood glucose levels in a series of 1989 studies (Kaplan et al, 1989).

Similarly, an approach known as 'autonomy support', based on self determination theory, has shown significant benefit in a variety of health outcomes such as HbA1c levels, attendance at alcohol treatment programmes and long term weight loss maintenance. Autonomy support is demonstrated when a health professional understands the person's perspective, acknowledges their feelings, and offers choices and relevant information (Williams et al, 1998; Ryan et al, 2008).

Other psychological evidence and models support this view. A series of studies of the empowerment model, which focuses on enabling people with diabetes to make choices and set goals for themselves, have shown improvements in blood glucose, lipids and importantly, self efficacy, ie the confidence to take action (Anderson et al 1995; Tang et al, 2005).

Acknowledging emotions is a key feature of PCP, but one which concerns many health professionals, due to worries about lack of time to deal with emotional issues and also the fear of 'opening a can of worms'. However, emotion is a key driver of behaviour, so is very relevant to an approach which is orientated towards an action plan. Contrary to the concerns expressed, Levinson et al (2010) found that where at least one emotional comment (known as a clue) given by a person in a consultation was acknowledged by the health professional, consultations were shorter, whilst they were longest when health professionals repeatedly missed or dismissed these clues.

The reasons why people do not always act on advice and how to communicate information more effectively are summarised by Myers and Abraham (2005). They describe the importance of information about treatment being tailored to a person's belief system. The benefits of detailed, step by step planning and advance problem solving to promote success in taking action are also cited.

The emphasis on self efficacy and empowerment in relation to effective learning is supported (Knight et al, 2006). Whilst acknowledging that more research is needed, in a review of educational interventions, these authors re-emphasised that programmes that concentrated on knowledge alone, were less effective in enabling people to self manage their condition than those which also incorporated behavioural and psychosocial components. Also emerging from the review was the observation that 'rigid dietary instruction and obedience training have no place in modern diabetes education' (p.497) and the observation that a change in health professionals' own behaviour may also be needed to achieve change among people with diabetes.

In relation to people receiving their results in advance of the consultation, as far back as 1982 Philip Ley identified the lack of evidence for any adverse effects of greater information sharing, including people being given information about test results or having access to their own case notes (Ley, 1982), and this is still true today. Health professionals are often more concerned than people themselves about sharing clinical information, an interesting situation given that it is very obviously the person's own information.

Sharing of test and investigation results may be the most novel component of PCP, and published evidence of its effectiveness is sparse so far. However, the Year of Care project report (Diabetes UK et al, 2011), and our own discussions in PCP training workshops with participants who have implemented results sharing, show that not only do people often welcome their results and the chance to plan their consultation in advance, this approach can also lead to some people attending their consultations again after a period of persistent absence. These reported experiences are supported by a recent trial in Ireland (Hong et al, 2010) which involved giving personalised clinical information to people, plus the chance to select topics to discuss in their consultation, whilst waiting for their diabetes clinic appointment. The results showed that these people participated significantly more than those in the control group, without extending the length of the consultation.

Helping people help themselves

One of the most recent additions to the literature in support of PCP is the document 'Helping people help themselves', which is a review of the evidence to support self management (de Silva, 2011). This review of hundreds of pieces of evidence emphasises the view that a range of strategies is more likely to promote self management than information-giving alone. It also identifies that behavioural approaches, including active goal setting and action planning, are important. A list of strategies that work well is included, headed by involving people in decision-making about their condition and care, emphasising problem-solving, and people developing care plans in partnership with health professionals (see Table 2 overleaf). All these aspects are integral to PCP.

In summary, this brief review of some of the current evidence which is relevant to PCP and its components, which is drawn from a wide variety of sources including medical, educational and psychosocial, shows that it has many benefits. These include more effective use of time, potential cost savings, improved outcomes and self efficacy for the person with a long term condition, and greater motivation and satisfaction for healthcare professionals.

Table 2: Strategies that work well to support self management (de Silva, 2011a)

- Involving people in decision making
- Emphasising problem-solving
- Setting goals and following up on how well they are achieved
- Care plans developed in partnership with health professionals
- Helping people to self-monitor their symptoms and know when to take action
- Motivating people to self manage using targeted approached and structured information and support
- Helping people manage the social, emotional and physical aspects of their condition
- Proactive follow-up
- Providing opportunities to share and learn from other service users

Chapter 3: Embedding PCP in health professional practice

This chapter looks at the implications of PCP for the practice of health professionals, and includes some reflective questions that you can use to reflect on your own thoughts and beliefs in relation to PCP.

PCP and health professional practice

Implementing PCP will probably require a change in behaviour for some, if not all, health professionals, to step away from being the person in charge and the chief decision-maker about people's health. PCP means sharing with people information about their condition which traditionally has been 'for your eyes only'. It means adopting a more facilitative approach in consultations, allowing the person to talk more, and focusing on emotional and social concerns as well as biomedical issues.

Changing practice as a health professional can be just as challenging as it is for anyone with a long term condition to change their behaviour. Familiar, well-rehearsed ways of doing things become habits, which can only be changed by paying attention and making a conscious effort to do something differently each time the behaviour arises. For example, if you are used to giving lifestyle advice based on biomedical test results, when you implement PCP you may need to consciously remember to wait to speak until you have heard what the person thinks about their own results. It can be hard to resist the urge to interrupt or offer your own opinion, and the philosophy of PCP means that your advice may not be relevant or even required at all. You won't always succeed in prioritising the person's opinion and decisions, especially at first.

The extent to which you want to change, and the value you see in changing, will influence how hard you are likely to work to adopt new practices. A starting point is to think about what your beliefs and attitudes are about your role and responsibility in healthcare, and the role and responsibilities of people with long term conditions.

Your training to become a health professional is likely to have focused more on the acute model of care than the approach to long term conditions discussed here, which is likely to result in you feeling responsible *for* the people you see, rather than responsible *to* them. This important distinction is emphasised by Bob Anderson and Marti Funnell in their description of empowerment, which has enormous similarity with the approach used in PCP. Table 3 on the next page contrasts the traditional and empowerment approaches to healthcare, and is adapted from their book, 'The Art of Empowerment' (Anderson & Funnell, 2005). This table can be a useful starting point if you wish to reflect on the practical implications of implementing PCP.

If you are committed to PCP, you will persist in your efforts to work in keeping with the philosophy, and in time, you will have adopted a new way of behaving, a new habit of collaborating.

Successful Diabetes Tip

Invest some time in considering the underlying approaches for acute health care and for PCP, and reflect on how your own approach may need to change

Table 3: Comparison of the traditional and empowering models of healthcare practice

Traditional Model	Empowerment Model
Illness is a physical ailment.	Illness has both physical and psychosocial aspects.
The health professional is the expert and is authoritarian within a consultation.	The health professional and person with the condition both bring their own expertise and have a democratic relationship within a consultation.
The health professional identifies what problems exist and what the person with the condition needs to know.	The person with the condition identifies what problems exist and what they need to know.
The health professional works out the solutions to problems and what the person with the condition should do, and is responsible for the outcome.	The person with the condition works out the solutions to problems and what they are going to do, the professional acts as a resource to help them set goals and develop a self-management plan. The person with the condition is responsible for their own actions and the outcomes that result.
The goal is behaviour change. Strategies are aimed at increasing compliance with recommended treatment. A lack of compliance is viewed as a failure of the person with the condition.	The goal is to enable the person with the condition to make informed choices. Strategies are used to help them experiment with behaviour changes of their choosing. Behaviour changes that are not adopted are viewed as learning tools to provide new information that can be used to develop future plans and goals.
Behaviour changes are externally motivated.	Behaviour changes are internally motivated.
The health professional is powerful, the person with the condition is powerless.	Both the health professional and the person with the condition are powerful.

Questions for reflection

This section outlines some of the principles of PCP and provides questions that you can use to identify how close your beliefs and attitudes are to those of a PCP approach.

Principle:

PCP recognises that the actions that the person with a long term condition takes, day to day are the major influence on the biomedical results.

Question for reflection:

How responsible do you feel you are for the outcomes that people achieve?

Principle:

PCP enables people to have information about their own condition prior to a consultation with a health professional.

Question for reflection:

What beliefs do you have about the ability of people with long term conditions to understand their results and make decisions based on them?

Principle:

The PCP process separates the gathering of information (through medical tests and investigations) from the consultation that discusses the results of these, to allow time to share the results and reflect on them. Both health professional and people undergoing the tests and investigations have access to the same information.

Question for reflection:

How committed are you to this idea?

Principle:

The PCP process invites people to reflect on their priorities for discussion in the consultation in relation to living with their condition, including emotional and social aspects as well as physical.

Question for reflection:

How comfortable are you with a consultation that prioritises the thoughts, feelings and concerns of the person with a long term condition?

Principle:

The PCP process means that the person with the long term condition does most of the talking during a consultation and decides for themselves what further information they need.

Question for reflection:

How skilled are you in active listening and being able to resist advice-giving?

Principle:

PCP results in an action plan, or care plan, which is based around the goals of the person with the long term condition.

Question for reflection:

How comfortable are you with a consultation where the person may choose goals and actions that would not be your choice or recommendation?

Just like any other change, being committed to the ideas underlying PCP is fundamental to its implementation. Your reflections might lead you to want to find out more about the person centred approach or talk with your colleagues, others or explore the perceptions of people with long term conditions before you feel ready to adopt this new approach and system of care.

Section two

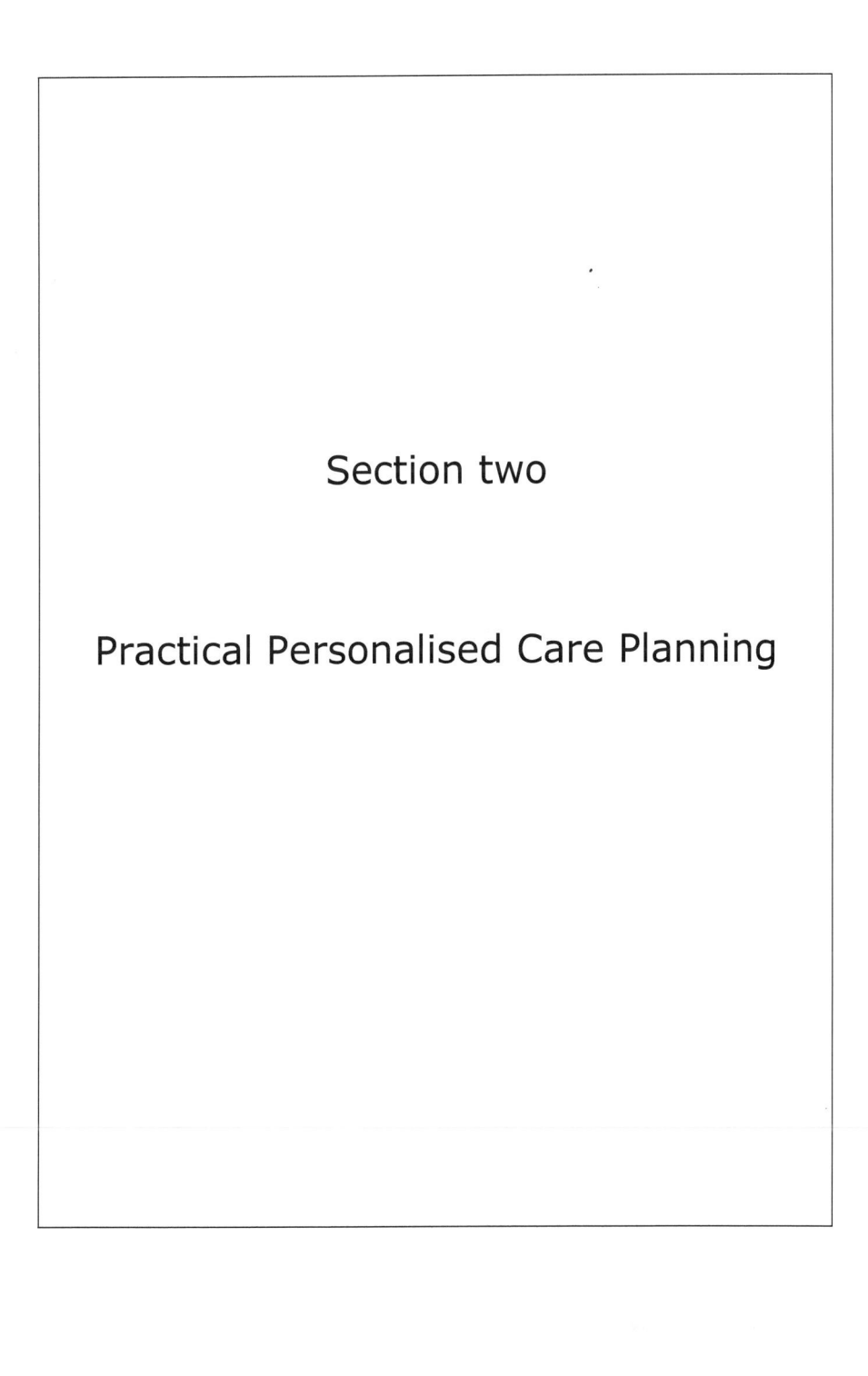

Practical Personalised Care Planning

Chapter 4: Preparation for introducing PCP

This chapter discusses some of the options you have in deciding how to implement PCP, and also how you might raise awareness about the change in your system of care, with a particular focus on preparing people with long term conditions.

PCP implementation strategy options

When you are starting to implement PCP, it is important to note that there isn't a single way that will suit all areas. It can be used simply within your own service, either by you as an individual for the people you see, or across your service, such as within a general practice or a whole clinic setting. Alternatively, it can be used across a whole locality.

Another aspect to consider is whether PCP will be tried out initially on a small group of individuals, whether it will be introduced for everyone with a specific condition, or whether it will be introduced for all people with long term conditions.

Whichever way you decide to implement PCP, you are likely still to need to consider doing this in a range of ways, in order to capture each person's particular needs. By its very nature, PCP is not a 'one size fits all' process! However, the philosophy and principles discussed earlier in this book apply to any way that you decide to implement PCP, and also the main components outlined in the flow diagram on page 14 need to be included.

Raising awareness

Whatever way you decide to implement PCP, for example as a whole process or by experiment with a small part such as receiving their results in advance, preparing people for the change in their system of care is vital. Something unusual happening without any warning can cause people anxiety and confusion, which could then limit their understanding about what the change is for.

The more you can manage people's expectations in relation to PCP, the more they will be able to play a full part in the process and the smoother your implementation of the approach will be.

> **Successful Diabetes Tip**
> People will find it easier to engage and participate in PCP if they have been provided with clear information about it in ways they can understand

It's possible that not everyone will welcome or accept a change in the way their care is provided, or even take notice of your efforts at advance preparation. Accepting that people are entitled to choose not to participate is an important part of the philosophy of PCP. However, it is important that everyone gets a choice, rather than assumptions being made by health professionals about whether different individuals are suitable for the process. Also, ensuring that the language and terminology you use in your awareness-raising materials enables people to feel they are being invited rather than forced to experience a new way of providing a service and is a strategy likely to reduce any resistance or concern for people.

> **Successful Diabetes Tip**
> You may need several months of raising awareness if you are planning to implement PCP across a locality, to give time for everyone to be informed

Table 4 overleaf shows some effective ways you could use to prepare people for a change to PCP.

Table 4: Ways of preparing people with long term conditions for a change in their process of care

* Explaining directly to people with long term conditions, getting their views and answering questions, for example in a focus group or by visiting a support group meeting
* Informing the relevant support organisations for the long term conditions, so that they can cascade information to their members
* Talking about the changes at a consultation and letting people know that next time (for example), they will be invited to 2 separate appointments, or receive a reflection invitation, or simply that they will have the chance to ask questions first when you meet again
* Sending an individual letter, email or DVD to all people concerned to explain what changes to expect
* Having a letter or DVD available at the clinic for reception staff to offer to people affected by the change or on request following advertising
* Using notice boards and computer screens in the clinic area to advertise the change, using words, pictures and diagrams
* Placing information on your service or organisation Internet site
* Using information leaflets from the NHS or Department of Health about PCP and informing people of the website addresses so they can find further information

Chapter 5: PCP interventions

This chapter discusses the steps that need to be taken to implement PCP, starting with ways that you can ensure that any tests and investigations relevant to the condition are carried out and shared with people, along with an invitation to reflect and consider their priorities before the PCP consultation. The PCP consultation model is shown and described in detail, along with details of the skills that are needed to hold this person centred consultation.

Tests and investigations prior to the PCP consultation

People having access to information about their health before their review appointment is one of the key aspects of making PCP a success. To achieve this, administrative changes are likely to be needed. Depending on the type of condition, people may need to attend for an additional appointment for investigations and blood tests, which may include aspects such as blood pressure checks, or foot checks for people with diabetes, so that all the relevant information is gathered. It may also be necessary to gather information from elsewhere, for example, if there is a district-wide screening system such as retinal screening in diabetes.

As an example, many people with diabetes already have blood tests taken in advance to check cholesterol, HbA1c and renal abnormalities, and other tests, such as blood pressure and a foot examination are taken at the time of the consultation. In the PCP approach, all these tests would be taken in advance, rather than being included in the PCP consultation, so that people have time to see and consider the results.

Some long term conditions do not have any particular tests needed in advance of the consultation and others have some for which a result on the day is necessary. You will need to consider what needs to be done for each long term condition, and how you can ensure there is time for the results to be obtained and shared in advance of their PCP consultation. If the condition requires tests to be carried out on the day of the consultation, it is useful to consider how you can provide people with time to think about their results. For example, could a test be taken earlier on the day of the consultation and the result made available for the person to reflect upon in time?

Whatever the particulars of the tests being taken, you will need to make arrangements for the clinical information to be collected. Table 5 shows some of the steps that may need to be taken to achieve this.

Table 5: Ways of organising the appointment for tests and investigations

* Involve people with long term conditions in decisions about how the clinic system might be organised
* Hold a meeting with colleagues to share your ideas and consider a range of possibilities
* Consider 'who does what' in your existing system and if there are opportunities for role re-design. For example, could a health care assistant become trained in taking blood or performing a diabetes foot check?
* Adapt appointment times so that staff with relevant skills are available. For example aligning a practice nurse clinic with a phlebotomy clinic to be able to take additional tests or examinations when people attend for their blood tests
* Consider if it is possible for people to take some measurements themselves at home, such as their weight, height, waist circumference and body mass index (BMI), to add to the list of results taken at the test appointment
* Revise the clinic system completely, to provide 2 appointments per person. This could be piloted to gauge its effectiveness

Successful Diabetes Tip

Consider expanding an existing role or service rather than creating a whole new system for completing tests and investigations in advance

Preparing for the PCP consultation

Without doubt, the biggest innovation brought by PCP is the opportunity it gives to people with long term conditions to reflect on their test results and their priorities in advance of the PCP consultation. This really brings to life the person centred approach. For this aspect to be implemented you will need to consider how to present the results and their explanation, how people will access them and how people might be encouraged to bring their reflections to the PCP consultation.

It's important to note that both the test results, and the invitation to reflect on what the person would like to discuss and ask in the consultation, are tools rather than end products in themselves. They do not have to be highly designed or expensively produced but they do have to be meaningful and well thought out.

Firstly, the results need to be presented in a useful way. Some people may prefer a factual approach with specific numbers and explanations; others may simply want to know what their results mean in general terms. Pictorial representations can be useful, for example using a colour coded system such as traffic light colours or cartoon depictions of smiley faces or thumbs down. The results need to be able to meet everybody's needs.

An explanation of what the test is for and an indication of the target range is essential. People will be used to receiving information directly from their health professional, including an interpretation of whether their results are in a healthy range or not. But it is important for the information about the target range to be delivered as factual information, so that the person with the condition can do the comparison between their results and the target ranges. So, for example, the message of 'your blood pressure is too high' is replaced with a message about 'a blood pressure of xxxx or below reduces your risk of developing a heart condition or having a stroke'.

There are a number of ways that have already been developed of providing results to people. Finding out what is already available and using 'off the shelf' versions (as found in the resources in chapter nine), or creating something new to meet the specific needs of your local population, are equally valid ways forward. If you are creating something new, gathering views from people who will be receiving and using the documents is essential.

Similarly, the invitation to reflect on concerns and priorities in advance of the consultation needs careful consideration. Again, there are 'off the shelf' examples or you can develop your own to meet the needs of people in your locality.

The extent to which people with long term conditions will engage with assessing and considering their results and planning for the consultation will depend, in part, on how well prepared they are to expect to do this. This emphasises the strong link between raising awareness and expectation beforehand, as already discussed, and participating in the results reflection.

In terms of people accessing their results in advance of their PCP consultation, this can be done in a wide variety of ways. For some, receiving information by post will be the best way but others may prefer to collect their results, receive them by telephone or fax or via email or a personalised health Internet site. Enabling people to choose how they receive their results and reflection invitation will increase the chances of them being well prepared for the PCP consultation.

There are some administrative practicalities in relation to collating and distributing results and these will need to be worked out. Examples include identifying who will create the documents and what resources will be needed, such as a colour printer or dedicated space. Table 6 shows a variety of ways you could implement results sharing and invitation to reflect on priorities for the PCP consultation.

> **Successful Diabetes Tip**
>
> Make sure that the way you present test results and reflection invitations caters for the varying needs of people in your local population

Table 6: Ways to share results prior to the PCP consultation

- Work with other relevant members of your team to create an administrative pathway for the results-sharing and the invitation to reflect, including which staff will be involved and what responsibilities they will have
- Collect some examples of results-sharing documents and show them to people with long term conditions to get their views so that you can customise them to your local needs
- Start small: offer a few people their results in advance of their next appointment, using a variety of ways of presenting them, and invite them to give you feedback
- Work with people who speak different languages or who have language difficulties to find out what method of presenting the information would be useful to them
- Identify what will work practically in terms of distributing results. For example, posting is efficient but can be expensive; people collecting their own results supports self-responsibility but may be hard in practice for some; electronic transfer is quick and cheap but may not be accessible for all
- Remind people that they are invited to reflect and prepare for the consultation, but it is not obligatory or a form of homework to please the health professional
- Ensure people know who to contact if they are alarmed or concerned at any stage of the process

The PCP consultation

Whilst it is important to prepare for using a PCP approach as already discussed, this will all be a waste if the PCP consultation itself is didactic, dictatorial or disempowering. This section looks in detail at the PCP consultation and the skills you need to use to ensure it is collaborative, including how to approach goal setting and action planning, which tend to be the least familiar aspects.

The PCP consultation is a person centred, collaborative encounter which gives equal importance to the views and opinions of both the person and the health professional. One of the things that differs in a PCP consultation (as opposed to a traditional consultation) is the recognition that it is the decisions the person makes in the consultation, and the actions they decide to take, that influence their health outcomes. This applies regardless of what actions you as a health professional wish them to take, so a key principle to keep in mind is that your view is only one side of the story.

Many health professionals believe that adopting a person centred approach means that somehow their own opinions and concerns matter less (see chapter eight), but this not the case and people wish to hear your views and specialist perspective in a consultation. However, your information and opinion can often be more useful when it adds to or clarifies something the person is already wondering about. For example, someone who comes to their consultation concerned about their high blood cholesterol levels or increasing weight might be wondering how they could go about improving these. The point at which they themselves identify this is when the medical or clinical information you offer will be most useful to them.

A five step person centred model of consulting

The following five step model, shown in Table 7, is based on the Michigan Empowerment Model developed for diabetes care. Person centred models like this are advocated throughout the literature for PCP consultations.

Table 7: A five step, person centred consultation model

Step 1: Identify the issue of most concern
Step 2: Explore feelings, beliefs and values
Step 3: Consider options and define goals
Step 4: Make a plan
Step 5: Review and reflect

Step 1: Identify the issue of most concern to the person

People tend to act in accordance with their concerns, so finding out what they are most concerned about makes sense. Their main concern may be related to their physical health or it may be a social, family or emotional issue. Receiving medical results and the invitation to reflect on priorities for the consultation in advance makes it easier for the person to clarify what concerns are most important.

It's unlikely that your concerns will be the same as the person's. For example, you may wish to focus on a raised cholesterol or blood pressure reading, but the person may be most concerned about another medical test or their sick relative, potential job loss or family difficulties. This does not mean that your concern is not important, but that it is not the *most* important.

Identifying the issue of most concern does not mean that you have to be an expert in that aspect or have the solution to it, especially if it is not medically related, for example money worries or family breakdown. Clarifying and acknowledging the issue and helping the person identify for themselves how they can move forward about it can itself be extremely therapeutic.

Step 2: Explore feelings, beliefs and values

As with concerns, people act in accordance with their feelings, beliefs and values, including cultural norms. Exploring the background to someone's concerns in relation to feelings, beliefs and values can give clarity to both you and the person. Behaviour that is hard for you to understand, for example not taking medication or not making health related lifestyle changes, often has its roots in a person's beliefs about its value or effect or habits that are well rehearsed and seem too hard to change.

The emotional state a person is experiencing can also make a huge difference. Not only can everyday worries get in the way of concentrating on health issues, but also depression, anxiety and mental health problems often coexist with other long term conditions. This makes it much harder to self manage as effectively as a person would like. As the evidence in chapter two showed, simply acknowledging emotional cues in a consultation can be very important, even if there is no obvious solution or way forward.

Step 3: Consider options and define goals

The most important aspect of this step is to enable the person to create and consider options for dealing with their situation. Sometimes this will be straightforward, especially if the person has already considered options prior to the consultation or if one option comes readily to the fore. At other times there will be a range of possibilities and deciding will be more difficult.

Once an option is settled upon, the goal, or goals, need to be set by the person, as they are much more likely to work towards their own personal goal than one set for them by you or someone else.

In the PCP consultation, the person with the long term condition will have had the opportunity of considering their personal goals prior to the consultation, so may already have goals in mind on attending their appointment, which makes for much more effective use of consultation time. The information sharing discussions that precede the goal setting stage of the consultation will help to refine and clarify the goals.

Discussing the goals in detail, including what behaviours or feelings would accompany them will enable both parties to have a clear vision of what the person is aiming for.

Examples of questions to find out someone's options and goals are:
- ✸ What options do you see for moving forward?
- ✸ What would you like to achieve?
- ✸ What would be your ideal situation?

Inviting the person with the long term condition to assess how important any goal they have is to them, and also how confident they are that they will achieve it, will give an insight into the likelihood of it being achieved.

In general, if you ask someone to rate their goal on an importance or confidence rating of 0-10 scale (where 10 is high), any rating of seven or above shows a high commitment to the goal and an increased likelihood of achieving it. A lower score doesn't mean it won't be achieved, but can indicate that there are too many barriers in the way. If a person suggests a low importance or confidence score, it is important to discuss what these barriers might be, in order to plan how to deal with them, thus making them less of a problem.

If the importance or confidence ratings are very low, it may be that a different or less ambitious goal is needed, so that one can be chosen that has a higher likelihood of being achieved.

Examples of questions you can use to assess importance and confidence are:

* What's the most important issue to you at the moment?
* How important is it to you to address this (aspect of condition) at the moment?
* On a scale of 0-10, how confident would you say you are about reaching your goal?

Step 4: Make a plan

Action planning is an essential step in a PCP consultation. In PCP, the action plan forms the care plan (or other term such as health plan or support plan). It is important that the action plan contains actions for both you and the person to undertake.

Actions that meet the criteria of SMART are much more likely to be successful than vague ones, so taking time to clarify all these aspects is a worthwhile investment. The SMART acronym stands for the following:

* S = Specific
* M = Measurable
* A = Achievable Action
* R = Realistic
* T = Timescaled

For example, the action plan 'I will eat less fattening foods in the next few months' sounds admirable but is not SMART. A SMART action plan would be 'every Tuesday for the next month I will eat fruit instead of my usual chocolate cake and cream at lunchtime'. Working on the steps that will help achieve the goal, and making them SMART, will result in successful action plans.

The same SMART principles apply to your own actions. A vague plan to 'refer to the podiatrist at some point' or 'I will check your blood pressure again soon' are much more likely to be achieved if they are altered respectively to, 'I will send the referral to the podiatrist by email this afternoon' and 'I will check your blood pressure two weeks today'.

You can explore potential barriers to the plan and rate your confidence in it in the same way as described for goal setting. This will make it even more likely to succeed.

Examples of questions you could use during the action planning process are:

* What would you need to do to get started on your action plan?
* What support do you need to put your action plan in place?
* What might stop you taking the action you want?
* On a scale of 0-10 (high), how likely is it that you will be able to carry out your plan?

Step 5: Review and reflect

This fifth step recognises that a key feature of PCP is the opportunity to reflect on progress so far and consider new priorities. The details of the action plan will determine whether reflection and review take place prior to the next consultation or contact, or at the start of it.

Not every action needs reflection by yourself and the person together. For example, in relation to behaviour change activities that the person might undertake, the most important factor is self monitoring by the person. If the action plan includes how the person would like to review any changes they have decided upon, this will make it very clear and also makes changes much more likely to be implemented.

Skills for person centred consulting

A key skill that is needed for put the PCP consultation to take place is active listening. Listening involves not talking, but not talking doesn't on its own mean that you are listening. It is possible to hear without listening, or simply be waiting to say something, or tapping information into the computer while waiting for the other person to finish what they are saying!

This section provides an overview of active listening skills, which you can use in the PCP consultation to really listen to what the person is saying and make sure that what you say and do is helpful and effective. These skills are an essential part of implementing a person centred approach and are helpful in all forms of communication.

Open questions

Open questions give people the opportunity of speaking or answering questions from their point of view, rather than just giving specifics that you might want. To use them effectively, the question needs to be asked and then you need to stop talking to allow people to answer. Open questions are particularly useful at the start of a consultation, when you are trying to find out the person's view of their results or their priorities for the discussion.

Examples of open questions are:

* How are you?
* What are you finding difficult just now?
* What do you think about your results?
* What questions have come up for you as you planned for our meeting?
* Which aspects of your condition would you most like us to talk about today?
* Tell me what you been thinking about in relation to your condition?
* Can you describe how your condition affects your day to day life?

It is also important to ensure that you don't immediately close down an open question by providing the potential answer yourself, for example "How are you? Alright?"

Reflection

Reflection is concerned with *feelings*, and generally means trying to explore what is behind what people are saying, either verbally or non-verbally. It needs to be tentative to give the person the opportunity of disagreeing if it is not how they are feeling.

Examples of reflective questions are:

* Does that mean you're fairly worried about this?
* It sounds as though this has made you very angry – is that right?
* You looked sad when you talked about your mother's illness – is that how you feel?

Paraphrasing

Paraphrasing is concerned with the *content* of the conversation, and is a summary of what someone has said. This will ensure that you both agree on what has been said and what is meant by it, and by identifying that you have heard what has been said, it will help someone to move on in their thinking.

Examples of paraphrasing are:

* So, what I'm hearing is that your pain has been getting gradually worse over the last few weeks
* It sounds like it's been difficult to deal with looking after yourself whilst your mum has been ill
* So you haven't been able to get much sleep and this has led to the exhaustion that you're now feeling

Concreteness

This is used to encourage someone to be more specific when they are being vague, for example using words like 'everyone', 'things' or 'people'.

Examples of vague statements and potential concrete open questions in response are:

* 'No-one understands me.' 'Who is it exactly that doesn't understand you?'
* 'It's all getting too much for me.' 'What is happening in your life to make you feel like that?'
* 'It's just the usual things that are getting in the way.' 'What specifically is causing you the most difficulty?'

Summarisation

This includes a summary of both the *content* of what has been discussed and the *feelings* that the person is experiencing. It could be used at the beginning of a consultation to sum up where things are at the moment, in the middle of the consultation, or at the end.

Examples of summarising statements are:

* When we last met, we talked about xxx and xxx and you decided xxx
* We've talked about three different options so far, and you have said you feel ready to make a decision
* You've identified that you want to lose weight, and that you feel determined to make it happen

Silence

Silence on your part can often replace an open question. The main advantage of silence is that it gives a person time to think about their reply, and also indicates that you are really listening and focused on the person. A silence accompanied by a nod, or enquiring look, shows that you are actively listening.

Silences rarely occur or last in consultations, but they can have a calming effect and help people to really think about their situation to be able to make productive decisions about how to move forward.

Examples of how you can use silence are:

* Holding back from asking your next question for a few seconds, to give the person time to add to what they have just said
* Refraining from reading notes or looking at the computer screen while you are waiting for the person to say something
* If the person does not start to talk, asking them to tell you what they are thinking about will provide them with a prompt

Non-verbal communication

This skill includes being aware of expressions, actions and positions of your body and those of the person you are consulting with. They can be very powerful, even though they are often unconscious to both parties. Particular aspects to be aware of include the positions you are sitting in, facial expressions of approval or disapproval, showing interest or looking bored, and movements such as tapping or fidgeting.

Being more aware of the non-verbal communication of the person you are consulting with can be helpful, especially when there is discrepancy between what they are saying and how they appear, such as a person who says 'fine' when you ask them how they are, but they have tears in their eyes or sit with their arms and legs tightly crossed. Providing comments on what is happening and inviting responses can help the person to acknowledge what they are feeling, and to discuss it with you.

Examples of commenting on non-verbal communication are:

* You look really tense
* You have a worried look on your face
* I can see you relaxed a bit when we talked about your results

Additional tips for successful PCP consultations

These additional tips will help you to make your PCP consultations even more successful:

* After an open question, leave time for a full answer, even if this means a few seconds of silence
* Think of yourself as 'supporting' rather than 'teaching' or 'educating' or 'advising'
* Offer information and resources, rather than assuming what's needed
* Think of goal setting and action planning as processes in the consultation, not tasks for you to achieve.
* Talk with people, not at them
* Change how you phrase questions, for example changing from "I think…" to "what do you think?", or from "you should…" to "one option is…". This makes your consultations instantly more person centred.

Section three

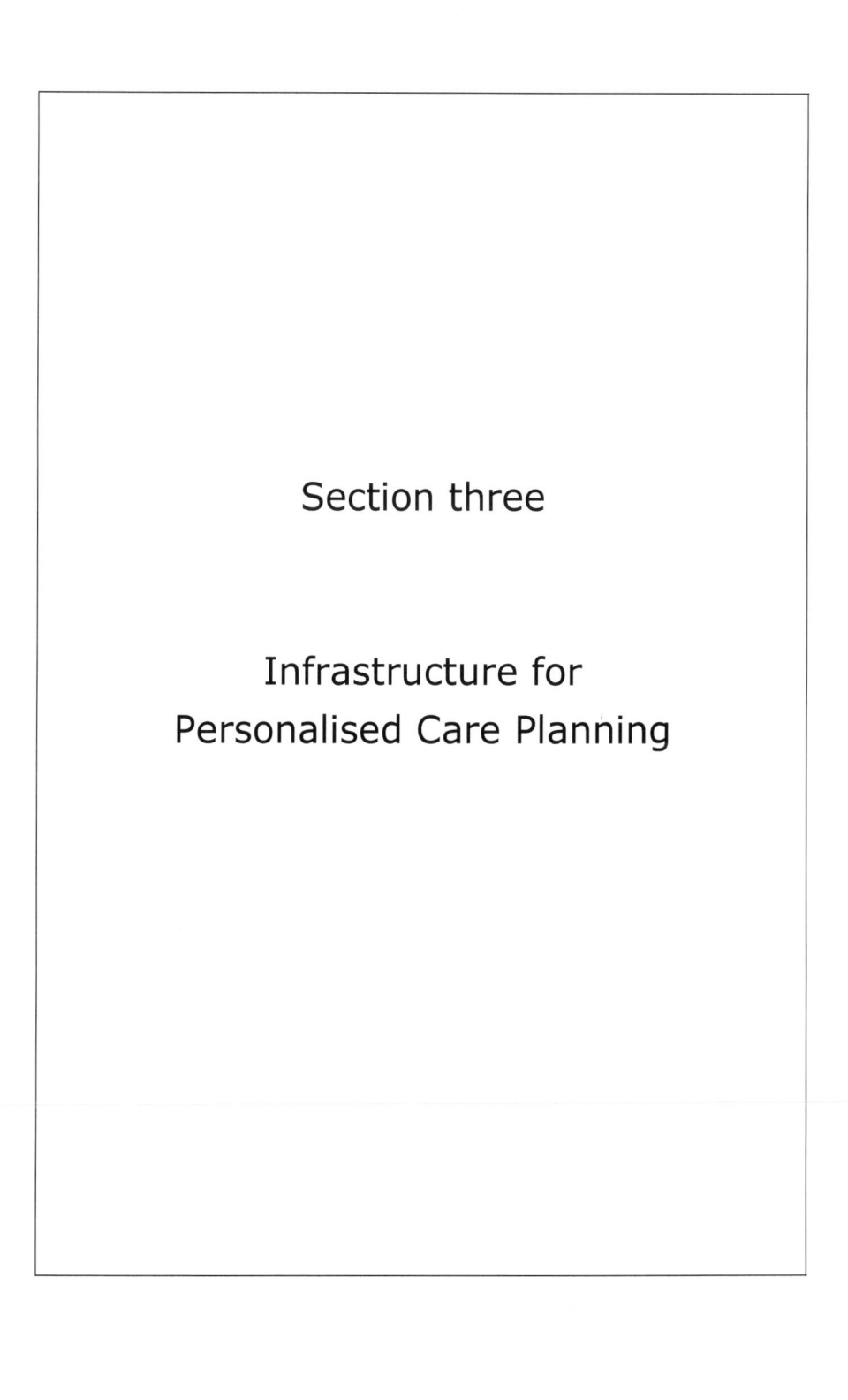

Infrastructure for Personalised Care Planning

Chapter 6: Documentation

This chapter looks at what documentation you will need at each stage of PCP and gives some examples of wording for letters and results sharing.

An overview of PCP documentation

When you are implementing PCP, there are a number of documents that you will need as a minimum, including printed documents and computer templates. The documents are listed below, and tables 9 to 11 provide some examples that you can adapt for your own use:

* An invitation letter for tests and investigations prior to the PCP consultation

* A follow up letter for if there is no reply or the person is not able to attend

* A document which enables you to share test results and other clinical information, which should also include general targets for people to compare with, and an invitation to reflect on the results and consider their priorities before their PCP consultation

* Documentation to record the outcome of the PCP consultation, ie the action (care) plan, both in the medical records and as a copy that can be held by the person with the condition

Some documentation will be available as part of your everyday systems, but others you will need to create, either from those available already or specifically for your population. One way to identify the documentation you need is to use the PCP process to look at each stage. Table 8 on the next page shows an example of what this might look like.

> **Successful Diabetes Tip**
> Identifying all the documentation needed helps to make implementing PCP very straightforward

Table 8: A flow chart of the PCP process, with the documentation underlined at each stage

> Give information to people with long term conditions personally, about the changes they can expect to their consultation and the system of care, through <u>letters (by post or email), leaflets and information boards in the practice, and information attached to repeat prescriptions</u>

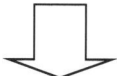

⬇

> Send a <u>letter of information</u> before the first appointment for any tests or investigation, about 4 weeks prior to the PCP consultation. <u>Keep attendance log</u>

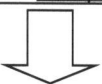

⬇

> <u>Follow up letters, emails or telephone calls</u> to people who have not been able to attend for tests and investigations and offer another appointment

⬇

> Send out (where relevant) the <u>results of tests and investigations, with an explanation of their meaning, and an invitation to reflect</u> on what topics to cover in the consultation

⬇

> Capture PCP consultation, including goal setting and action planning on a <u>computer template</u>

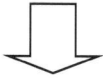

⬇

> Document <u>action plan</u> in electronic notes, with copies for the person (if wanted) by <u>letter, email or electronic log</u>

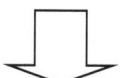

⬇

> Activate personalised care (action) plan, including review as agreed

Wording for appointment invitations

The wording for your letter of appointment will depend on how your appointment system usually works, for example, do you want the person to be given their first appointment, to be given the first appointment and then make the second when they attend, or whether you wish to invite people to make an appointment themselves at a time which is convenient to them. Table 9 provides an example of the type of information you may include in the invitation letter.

Table 9: Example of wording of invitation to PCP appointments

Dear

Your regular review of your (long term condition) is due at the (venue name). This review is a chance to discuss your condition and how you are managing it and to make a personalised care plan for the future.

We would like to offer you these two appointments:

Appointment one: On (date) at (time), a 20 minute appointment to have your routine tests and investigations.

On (date) at (time), to discuss your results and make a personalised care plan.

If the dates or times are inconvenient to you, please let us know so that we can rearrange them.

Between the two appointments, we will send you the results of your tests plus the target values to compare them with, and this letter will also invite you to think about the results and what concerns and questions you wish to discuss.

Please bring the following with you to the first appointment (add information)

We are looking forward to seeing you

Yours sincerely

Wording for results letters

It is important to carefully plan the content of the letter containing test results and clinical information, to ensure that people have the best possible chance of understanding that information, and also that they are prepared for being more involved during their PCP consultation. Table 10 shows an example of a letter which encompasses both those aspects.

Table 10: Results letter example

Dear

Following your recent appointment, please find your results below, together with the normal ranges so that you can compare them. It also gives you ideas of ways you can prepare for your review appointment on (date and time).

Results

(Test   Result   Normal range   Explanation)

(Test   Result   Normal range   Explanation)

Preparing for your review

These questions will help you prepare for the discussion you will have with your health professional at your review. Please make a note of any answers or other thoughts you have, and bring these to your consultation so that they can be included in the discussions about your (long term condition) and can help us to agree a really useful action plan.

* What are you most concerned about in relation to living with your (long term condition)?
* What questions have you got about your test results?
* What would you like more information about, and what format of information would suit you best (eg booklets, internet sites, videos etc)
* What support would help you in living with your (long term condition)?
* What aspects of your condition would you really like to sort out the most in the near future?

It can also be useful to include some aspects of living with a long term condition, both in relation to the specific condition and also general aspects that apply to many conditions. These can then act as prompts for the person to think about. It is important, however, that any list you include is not seen as providing the only options that people might want to talk about. Table 11 provides ideas on how that can be achieved.

Table 11: Prompts to include with results letter

Here are some aspects of living with your condition that you might want to discuss. Make a note of any that you would to talk about when we meet, including what exactly you need to talk about.

Pain control

Tiredness

Eating and drinking healthily

Physical activity and moving about

Family and social life

Stress, anxiety or depression

Monitoring your condition

Taking medicines

You may also have other aspects that are not listed here. Please use this space to make a note of them here, so that we can include them in the discussion at your next consultation:

Documenting the care plan

Before the PCP consultation, most of the clinical data, such as blood pressure and smoking status, will have been entered as part of the data collection process. It will also be possible to document some of the information gained during the PCP consultation using your existing system. But it is important to ensure that the specifics of the care planning process are recorded in a way that makes them easy to recall. These include the individual's main concerns and priorities in terms of their care, their own specific goals, and their action plan. Table 12 overleaf shows an example of the format of a care plan, although you may prefer to develop your own.

A useful aspect to help ensure the care plan really belongs to the person is to ask them to complete it themselves. Some might prefer to use their own system, such as a notebook, diary or mobile device. The more ways you can find for someone to be involved in creating their own, personally meaningful action plan, the more likely it is to be implemented and shared at subsequent visits.

The PCP approach allows for the fact that the person's action plan is just that – their own. In this way it is a different concept from a 'patient held record', often used for recording and communication between health professionals. The PCP care plan does not have to be carried or returned unless the person chooses, although it is important to keep the information in the medical notes for medico-legal purposes, to ensure any health professional actions are carried out, and for reflection at subsequent consultations.

Successful Diabetes Tip

The action plan belongs to the person with the long term condition, not the health professional

Table 12: Example of a personalised care plan

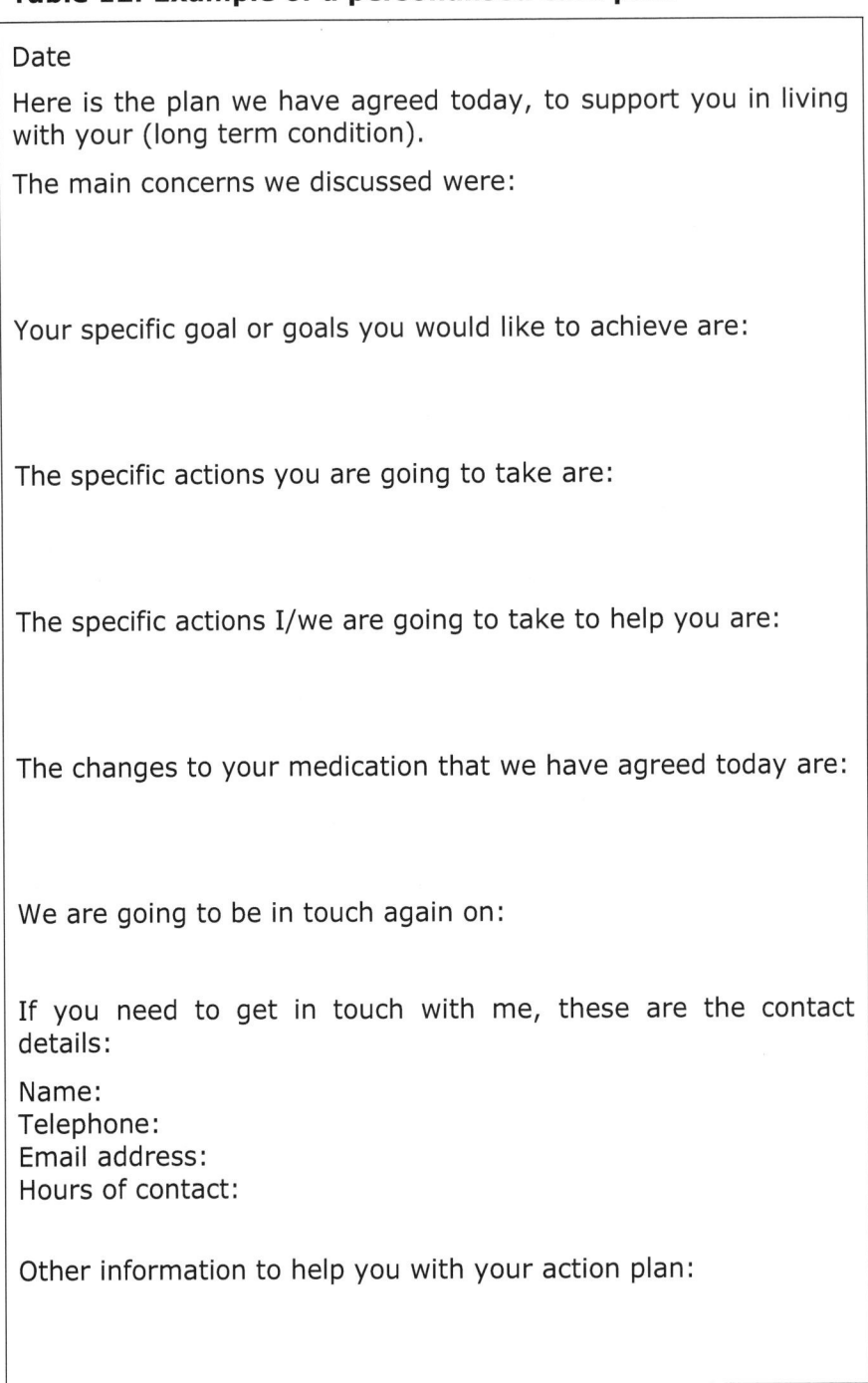

Date

Here is the plan we have agreed today, to support you in living with your (long term condition).

The main concerns we discussed were:

Your specific goal or goals you would like to achieve are:

The specific actions you are going to take are:

The specific actions I/we are going to take to help you are:

The changes to your medication that we have agreed today are:

We are going to be in touch again on:

If you need to get in touch with me, these are the contact details:

Name:
Telephone:
Email address:
Hours of contact:

Other information to help you with your action plan:

Chapter 7: Quality Assurance

Knowing how well you are doing in implementing PCP is essential. Having an efficient quality assurance (QA) system built in to your implementation will pay dividends. It will help with audit, show you the effectiveness of changes you are making to your clinical system and give you valuable feedback on your own behaviour changes, for example in your consultation style. This chapter describes the main principles of QA and offers some examples to get you started on how you could implement it in practice.

The main principles of quality assurance (QA)

* QA is about the process of delivery – in this case the PCP approach – rather than the outcomes
* QA is about continuously improving services rather than meeting an externally demanded target
* The purpose of QA is to identify whether a service is being delivered as specified, on different occasions and by different people
* QA consists of a list of standards for the service, in categories, and also a number of measures, which are the features that can be observed
* QA can be undertaken by an individual to assess their own practice, or internal (measured by other people within the organisation), or external (measured by someone from outside the service). An ideal QA system incorporates both internal and external observations.
* QA can be used to identify aspects of the service which are being delivered well, and also those which might be in need of further development.
* A regular review of the QA standards and measures being used is needed, to ensure they continue to be appropriate for the design of the service

Identifying QA standards and measures

To implement QA, it is important to create the standards to be achieved, plus measures that can be used to show that the standards have been achieved. This needs to happen for each part of the PCP approach, as outlined in table 8 on page 53. Table 13 below shows examples of two standards and their measures that you could put in place to prepare individuals for their PCP consultation.

Table 13: Example QA standards and measures for preparation for the PCP consultation

Standard	Measures
* Every person for whom it is relevant receives an appointment for routine tests and investigations	* A registration and recall system is in place * Appointments for tests are sent to each eligible person at least 4 weeks prior to their PCP consultation
* Before the PCP consultation, every person is encouraged to consider their concerns and wishes in relation to their care	* Appointment letters include questions for reflection on results, concerns and wishes in relation to their condition and care * At the beginning of the PCP appointment, the person is asked for their reflections and what they would like to achieve at this appointment.

It is also important that when assessing the standards and measures in practice, changes are made on the basis of what you find. Indication for the need to make changes would include finding that the measure is hard to assess in practice, if the standard seems unrealistic to achieve or if internal or external observers do not find the wording clear.

It is important too that the QA you use also assesses less formal aspects, such as what happens during a PCP consultation. Table 14 gives examples of consultation standards and measures that could be used for this.

Table 14: Example QA standards and measures for the PCP consultation

Standard	Measures
* Active listening skills are used by Healthcare Professionals (HCPs) during PCP consultations	* Open questions are used for more than 50% of the time. * HCP listens to the answers without interrupting. * HCP uses eye contact and nodding to encourage people to talk. * The content of the discussion and the feelings expressed by the person are paraphrased and reflected back to show understanding.
* Joint action planning is undertaken	* The person is able to identify SMART actions they will take and what support and help they need from their HCP. * The actions are documented in a way that accurately reflects what the person is going to do. * A confidence scale is used to assess the likelihood of the action plan being completed.

The QA process

Once you have identified standards and measures for each stage of the process, and you have made them as clear as possible, the next step is to develop some documentation to use by assessors for both internal and external QA. This should include the standards and measures, and also a recording method to identify whether they have been met, for example whether completely achieved, partly achieved or not achieved. There should also be space for comments, and for recording of specific examples that reflect the observer's decision. So in table 14, if the measure of 'HCP listens to the answers without interrupting' was only partly met, the example recorded might be 'when the person was talking about xxx, you interrupted them to say xxx'.

The observer, whether internal or external, should be someone who has a sound understanding of the principles of QA, as outlined on page 59. They should be provided with the standards, measures and recording documentation in advance of the assessment, so that they have time to digest the information, be clear about what they are looking for, and address any queries they might have.

It is also important to create a feedback system, so that discussion can take place between the observer and the people responsible for the section of the PCP process that is being observed. So for example if it was the consultation, then ensuring a time is arranged for feedback after the consultation, and preferably with a limited time interval, is recommended. Good practice for a feedback process includes:

* Firstly, offering the person responsible the opportunity to comment initially on whether they felt they had reached the standard or if there were any discrepancies

* Secondly, discussing the results in the order of 'what went well', 'what went less well', and 'what could be done differently'

Adhering to these principles means that the whole QA process is used as a helpful way of ensuring that PCP is being carried out and developed as intended.

Successful Diabetes Tip

Obtaining objective evidence and supportive feedback through QA is one of the best ways of learning and developing practice: be open to it

Section four

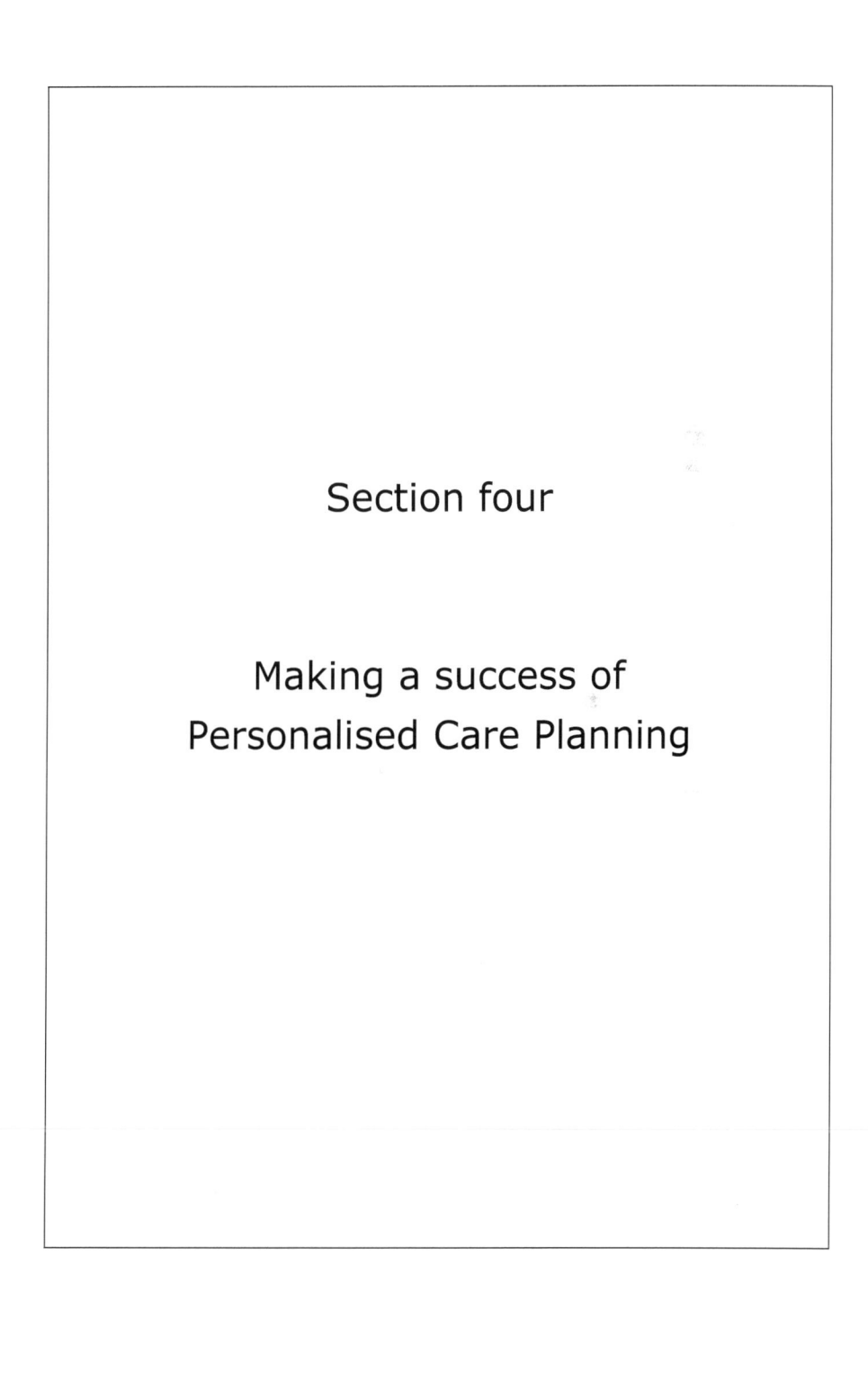

Making a success of Personalised Care Planning

Chapter 8: PCP concerns and questions

It is natural to have some concerns when you are embarking on a new venture, however committed you are to it. This chapter presents a range of common concerns that have been expressed by people new to implementing PCP, and offers some ideas and comments to address them. It also contains some frequently asked questions that may provide you with reassurance and inspiration!

PCP concerns

Won't people worry too much about their results if they receive them in advance of the consultation?

People are often extremely worried before their consultation anyway, partly because they fear being told 'bad news' about their results. Being prepared for and receiving the results in advance, along with an explanation of what they mean, means they have time to react to the information and work out what it means to them and what they want to discuss. Some people will decide they don't want this process, but the available evidence, both published and anecdotal, says that people welcome the chance to know their results and the process helps them to make decisions.

We've always used care plans – what's different about PCP?

The main difference is that the care plan arises from the joint conversation in the PCP consultation, focusing on the person's thoughts, beliefs and feelings about their condition and its care, and reflects the person's own goals and actions they have decided to take. A traditionally 'issued' care plan is one in which they generally had less input and decisions were made for them.

I find that people simply don't want to take responsibility for their condition

The bottom line is that people are already responsible for their condition day in, day out. PCP seeks to explore and support this responsibility rather than make people passive as in the traditional, or acute medical model.

What if people set goals that have nothing to do with their condition?

One way of thinking about a long term condition is that it is inextricably linked with a person's life, it is not a separate entity. People will act on their personal goals for their life, not those set by someone else. Goal-setting discussions may not obviously be about their condition, but will include implications for their condition, so are equally valid.

I don't think this would go down well with the people who come to our practice

Depending whether you feel committed or uncertain about adopting the philosophy of PCP will influence how likely you feel it will be successful. If you lack confidence in the approach or are unconvinced about using it, you are more likely to be worried about people you see regularly also being reluctant to accept a change to their usual system of care. If this is the case, working out what your objections are and addressing them, and if possible hearing from colleagues who have implemented PCP successfully, might help you feel more comfortable. As the underlying philosophy of PCP shows, you are unlikely to put it into practice just because someone else tells you to!

It can also be useful to ask the people with long term conditions whom you see regularly, about their views on becoming more involved. Asking them about their experiences, offering them opportunities to reflect before their consultations, or completing a questionnaire about their preferences will provide you with information about their thoughts and give you experience of the process, so you can then reflect on its success or otherwise. It is worth remembering that PCP has been introduced successfully and welcomed by people with long term conditions in all localities, including those which hold significant challenges such as cultural diversity or low health literacy.

Frequently asked questions

This section looks at some of the common questions about practically implementing PCP, and suggests ways they may be answered. There is also signposting to additional sources of information that you will find in chapter nine.

I'd like to try out sharing results in my practice but my colleagues aren't so keen. What can I do?

Rather than trying to convince them in words, one way to help others see the benefit of a change in practice is to experiment with it and present the results to them for their consideration. If you try results sharing with some people and document the effects of it, and their opinion about it, and the results are positive, then sharing this information will help your colleagues see how it works in a practical way. Also, finding out and addressing your colleagues' main concerns is important, as these are the ones they will act upon, just as the approach advocates for the PCP consultation.

Where do we find the time in our practice to allow for two appointments and all the paperwork that the PCP approach involves?

Implementing PCP may well require some extra time until the new process gets underway, for example to organise the two separate appointments. However, it might be helpful to add up all the time needed for your current system, from an administrative, clinical and, not forgetting, the person's own time. Then think about using this time differently – for example, the PCP consultation no longer requires you to perform any medical tests or examinations, or to explain the person's results to them, but can be used instead to focus on listening to them and helping them to make decisions. Also, you are inviting the person to use the time between appointments to consider their agenda for the PCP consultation, which may well lead to them making decisions in advance of the PCP consultation, rather than during it. You might even find the PCP consultation is shorter as a result!

Does the PCP consultation take longer if the person has the chance to talk more?

Not necessarily. A lot depends on how you set up the PCP consultation and agree together how to use the time. The important thing is for the person to share their views and reflections and for you to listen to these and respond, as described in chapter five. Sharing with the person how much time is available for the PCP consultation, either with their reflection invitation prior to the consultation or at the start is very helpful to them.

Uninterrupted, a person rarely speaks for more than two or three minutes, and using listening skills such as paraphrasing and reflection helps to make the conversation structured and helpful. The evidence to date suggests that using the PCP approach does not add to the consultation time.

What if people prefer me to tell them what to do rather than make their own decisions – that's a valid choice, isn't it?

People are often conditioned to expect a health professional to make decisions for them, because that is the traditional experience. Often, however, they have not chosen this approach, but have had to accept the power balance that is skewed towards the health professional. In PCP, they have the opportunity to participate and can, of course, say they do not want to take part. Yes, this is a valid choice. The difference is that they are actively making the choice in the context of PCP, rather than having the decision made for them.

Remember, though, that even if someone asks you to tell them what to do, this doesn't necessarily mean they will do what you have told them! It remains the case that away from the consultation room, they may decide to do something different that suits them better. They remain much more likely to implement a decision they make themselves, than one you make for them.

I would like to consult in a more person centred way. How can I get started?

Maybe start small? For example, introduce a few more open questions into your consultations, questions starting with 'what do you think about…' or 'tell me how you are feeling…' You can also use a bit more silence in consultations, to give someone time to think and reflect – just holding back for five seconds or so, can produce some remarkable discussions. With repeated practice, this method of consulting becomes more of a habit and you will add more and more to your consultation style.

You can also let people know that you are trying to find out more about what they think and feel, and encourage them to ask questions or bring information they wish to discuss with them to their next appointment.

PCP is a person centred approach, so implementing results sharing prior to the consultation, so you can discuss the results equally with someone in the consultation, would also be a positive step.

If you wish to know whether changes you make are effective, you could ask people who you have consulted with to complete a questionnaire such as the Health Care Climate Questionnaire (see Self-Determination Theory website on p.71). Finding out how people respond to your approach can be extremely valuable and motivating. Good luck!

Chapter 9: Additional resources

In addition to the references cited throughout the book, this chapter provides you with ways to find out more about aspects of personalised care planning that specifically interest you. The chapter is divided into sections, listed alphabetically. Each section contains relevant documents and web addresses, so that you can easily find the resources you are interested in. All websites and pages are correct at the time of going to press.

Long term conditions support and campaigning organisations

There are a wide range of organisations offering support to people living with a long term condition, brought together in one helpful directory.

Department of Health (2009). Directory of National Support and Information Services. Department of Health, London.
http://www.dh.gov.uk/en/Healthcare/Longtermconditions/yourhealth/DH_098342

PCP and Diabetes

Personalised Care Planning was first piloted in diabetes care, via the Year of Care project. There have therefore been a number of initiatives started up to support PCP in diabetes, many of which are also relevant to PCP for long term conditions in general. They provide guidance and resources that you can use in your own practice.

Duquemin A (2011). Year of Care: Pilot case studies. Diabetes UK, Department of Health, Health Foundation, NHS Diabetes.
http://www.diabetes.org.uk/Professionals/Service-improvement/Year-of-Care/

Healthcare Commission (now Care Quality Commission) Service Review of Diabetes (2007).
http://www.cqc.org.uk/usingcareservices/healthcare/patientsurveys/servicesforpeoplewithdiabetes.cfm

Lewis-Barned N, Mitchell J (2008). Commissioning quality care. Diabetes Update, Winter, p.28.

NHS Diabetes (2009). Resource for Commissioning Diabetes Services. http://www.diabetes.nhs.uk/commissioning_resource/

NHS Diabetes (2011). Year of Care website section.
http://www.diabetes.nhs.uk/year_of_care/

Walker R (2008). Putting care planning into practice. Diabetes Update, Spring, p.25.

Walker R, Akroyd T (2008). Care Planning – the essentials for getting started. Diabetes Update, Summer, p. 35.

PCP and long term conditions

As PCP has started to be adopted more widely, there are a number of national initiatives and documents that provide guidance and support for ways of engaging better with people with long term conditions.

Department of Health (2006) Supporting people with long term conditions to self care: A guide to developing local strategies and good practice.
http://www.dh.gov.uk/en/Publicationsandstatistics/Publications/PublicationsPolicyAndGuidance/Browsable/DH_4100317

NHS web pages for Long Term Conditions and Care Planning.
http://www.nhs.uk/planners/yourhealth/pages/careplan.aspx

NHS Information Centre for Health and Social Care. Patient Reported Outcome Measures (PROMs) (2011).
http://www.ic.nhs.uk/proms

NHS Primary Care Commissioning (2011). New Resources for Commissioning.
http://www.pcc.nhs.uk/new-commissioning-resources

Skills for Care (2007) Common Core Principles to support Self Care. Leeds. Skills for Care.
http://www.skillsforcare.org.uk/publications/publications_c.aspx

Person centred models and consultation skills

Much of the research on empowerment in diabetes has been carried out at the University of Michigan, who have published various books and also hold a lot of resources on their website, included in this section of the resources. There are also other models and resources for working in a more person centred way.

Anderson B, Funnell MM (2005). The Art of Empowerment, 2nd edition. American Diabetes Association, Alexandria. Currently out of print, but PDF copies available on request from enquiries@successfuldiabetes.com

Mason P, Butler C (2010). Health Behavior Change. Churchill Livingstone, London.

Michigan Diabetes Research and Training Center.
www.med.umich.edu/mdrtc

Self-Determination Theory Website, containing full information about the theory and survey instruments.
www.psych.rochester.edu/SDT/

Walker R (2008). Consulting to empower. Diabetes Update, Autumn, p.29.

Successful Diabetes resources

We offer a range of support resources for PCP, including explanation, training workshops and a discussion video.

Successful Diabetes (2010). SD Focus. Personalised Care Planning – an Introduction.
http://www.successfuldiabetes.com/contact-us/170

Successful Diabetes one-day interactive workshops to develop consultation skills for the PCP approach as well as comprehensive care planning training.
http://www.successfuldiabetes.com/contact-us/70-workshops

Successful Diabetes: Personalised Care Planning Video
http://www.youtube.com/user/SuccessfulDiabetes#p/a/u/1/B4o60ntJGeQ

UK health policy and PCP

'Your health, your way' is one of the key documents to look at if you want to know more about what's behind the more person-centred approach to long term conditions in the NHS today. There are also many other documents that have specifically focused on long term conditions, which can be accessed using the link provided.

Department of Health (2008) Your health, your way.
http://www.dh.gov.uk/en/Healthcare/Longtermconditions/yourhealth/index.htm

Department of Health (2010). A selection of key documents related to policy.
http://www.dh.gov.uk/en/Healthcare/Longtermconditions/Publicationsandpolicyguidance/index.htm

References

Anderson RM, Funnell MM, Butler PM, Arnold MS, Fitzgerald JT, Feste CC (1995). Patient Empowerment: Results of a randomized controlled trial. Diabetes Care, 17, 943-949.

Anderson B, Funnell MM (2005). The Art of Empowerment, 2nd edition. American Diabetes Association, Alexandria. Currently out of print, but PDF copies are available on request from enquiries@successfuldiabetes.com.

Department of Health (2010). Equity and Exellence: liberating the NHS.
http://www.dh.gov.uk/en/Publicationsandstatistics/Publications/PublicationsPolicyAndGuidance/DH_117353

Department of Health (2009). Supporting people with Long Term Conditions. Commissioning personalised care planning. A guide for commissioners.
http://www.dh.gov.uk/en/Publicationsandstatistics/Publications/PublicationsPolicyAndGuidance/DH_093354

Department of Health (2008). High Quality Care for All: NHS next stage review final report. Department of Health, London.

Department of Health (2006a). Our health, our care, our say.
http://www.dh.gov.uk/en/Policyandguidance/Organisationpolicy/Modernisation/Ourhealthourcareoursay/index.htm

Department of Health (2006b). Care Planning in Diabetes.
http://www.dh.gov.uk/en/Publicationsandstatistics/Publications/PublicationsPolicyAndGuidance/DH_063081

Department of Health (2002). National Service Framework for Diabetes: Delivery Strategy.
http://www.dh.gov.uk/en/Publicationsandstatistics/Publications/PublicationsPolicyAndGuidance/DH_4003246

Department of Health (2000). The NHS Plan: a plan for investment, a plan for reform. Department of Health, London.

De Silva, D (2011). Helping people help themselves: A review of the evidence considering whether it is worthwhile to support self-management. Health Foundation, London.
http://www.health.org.uk/publications/evidence-helping-people-help-themselves/

Diabetes UK, Department of Health, Health Foundation, NHS Diabetes (2011). Year of Care. Report of findings from the pilot programme. Diabetes UK, Department of Health, Health Foundation, NHS Diabetes, London.
http://www.diabetes.nhs.uk/year_of_care/

Diabetes UK (2009). Improving supported self-management for people with diabetes. Diabetes UK, London.

Health Foundation (2011). Year of Care.
http://www.health.org.uk/areas-of-work/programmes/year-of-care/

Hong YY, Lim YY, Lim SYA, O'Donnell M, Dinneen SF (2010). Providing diabetes patients with personalised written clinical information in the diabetes outpatient clinic: a pilot study. Diabetic Medicine, 27, 685-690.

Kaplan S, Greenfield S, Ware JE (1989). Impact of the doctor-patient relationship on the outcomes of chronic disease. In Roter D and Stewart M (Eds.), Communicating with Medical Patients, Sage Publications Inc, London.

Knight KM, Dornan T, Bundy C (2006). The diabetes educator: trying hard, but must concentrate more on behaviour. Diabetic Medicine, 23, 485-501.

Levinson W, Gorawara-Bhat R, Lamb J. (2010). A study of patient clues and physician responses in primary care and surgical settings. JAMA, 284, 8, 1021-1027.

Ley P (1982). Satisfaction, compliance and communication. British Journal of Clinical Psychology, 21, 241-254.

Myers L, Abraham C (2005). Beyond 'doctor's orders'. The Psychologist, 18, 680-683.

NHS (2011). NHS Choices website.
http://www.nhs.uk/Pages/HomePage.aspx

NHS Diabetes (2011). Year of Care website section.
http://www.diabetes.nhs.uk/year_of_care/

NHS Diabetes (2008). Partners in Care: a guide to implementing a PCP approach to diabetes care.
http://www.diabetes.nhs.uk/year_of_care/

NHS Primary Care Commissioning (2009). Outline Service Specification: Personalised Care Planning for People with Long Term Conditions.
http://www.pcc.nhs.uk/personalised-care-planning

NICE (2011). Diabetes in adults quality standard. NICE, London.
http://www.nice.org.uk/guidance/qualitystandards/diabetesinadults/diabetesinadultsqualitystandard.jsp

NICE (2009). Medicines Adherence. Clinical guideline 76. NICE, London.

Northern Ireland Department of Health, Social Services and Public Safety (2011). Living with Long term conditions: a policy framework (consultation Document). Northern Ireland Assembly, Belfast.

Ryan RM, Patrick H, Deci EL, Williams GC (2008). Facilitating health behaviour change and its maintenance: Interventions based on Self-Determination Theory. European Health Psychologist, 10, 2-5.

Scottish Government Health Delivery Directorate Improvement and Support Team Long Term Conditions Collaborative (2010). Improving Care Pathways: A collaborative resource to support partnerships. The Scottish Government, Edinburgh.

Tang TS, Gillard ML, Funnell MM, Nwankwo R, Parker E, Spurlock D, Anderson RM (2005). Developing a New Generation of Ongoing Diabetes Self-Management Support Interventions. The Diabetes Educator, 31, 91-97.

Welsh Assembly Government (2002). The National Service Framework for Diabetes (Wales). Cardiff. Welsh Assembly Government.

Williams G, Freedman ZR, Deci EL (1998). Supporting Autonomy to Motivate Patients with Diabetes for Glucose Control. Diabetes Care, 21, 1644-1651.

Thank you for buying this book, we hope you have enjoyed it and found it useful. We'd love to hear what you think about it so please post a review at www.lulu.com or complete our short survey at www.surveymonkey.com/s/9ZFZMWS

Please visit our website www.successfuldiabetes.com to see our ever expanding range of information and products.

The Successful Diabetes Team.